Classic Tales

Level 5

AF283928

# The Magic Brocade

*Retold by Sue Arengo*
*Illustrated by Nancy Lane*

##  Contents


| | |
|---|---|
| The Magic Brocade | 2 |
| Exercises | 28 |
| Glossary | 30 |
| About *Classic Tales* | 32 |

**OXFORD**
UNIVERSITY PRESS

Long ago, in a small village, a woman lived with her three sons. Her husband had died and now she was poor. Her house was old and dark, and many things were broken. But the woman was brave.

She was a weaver and she worked hard every day. She wove beautiful brocades. Each brocade took five days to weave. She worked all week, and every Saturday she went to the market to sell her brocade. Then she bought rice, vegetables, and flour. And every Sunday she had a rest.

One Saturday the woman was at the market as usual and she saw something. It was a picture of a house … a lovely white and gold house, with a beautiful garden. An old man was trying to sell it.

'How much is this picture?' she asked him.

'How much have you got?' he replied.

'All I have is three coins,' said the woman.

'Then that is all it costs,' he smiled.

The woman looked at the picture. She wanted it very much. She looked at it and thought for a long time. Then she said, 'Here!' and she dropped her last three coins into the old man's hand.

'It's yours,' he said.
'Good luck, woman!'

'What a lovely house!' the woman's sons cried.

'I want to live there!' said the youngest.

'So do we!' said his two older brothers.

'Copy it, Mother!' cried the youngest. 'Weave a copy! Weave it into a brocade!'

So the woman began to work. The next day was Sunday and she usually rested on Sundays. But this time she worked. She worked all day. It was not easy to copy the picture.

'Stop for lunch!' her sons said.

'I can't!' she replied. 'I must do this right. This is going to be my best brocade!'

The woman worked every day. She only slept for
a few hours each night. She was so interested in her
work, she could not stop. She thought about the
picture all the time. She wanted to make her brocade
as beautiful as the picture.

'Mother!' her sons cried. 'Stop! Have a rest! Let's go
for a walk!'

'No, my dears!' she said. 'Go for a walk without me
and get some wood for the fire, please.'

The woman had no time to clean the house or
cook the food. So her sons had to clean the house
and cook the food. The youngest son was happy
to help, but the other two became angry.

'Hurry up and finish that brocade, Mother!'
they said. 'There is no more money.
Soon there will be nothing to eat!'

'I'm busy!' she said. 'Go and
chop some wood! Go and sell
some wood at the market!'

The older brothers didn't like
chopping wood.

'It's too hot!' they said.

'I'll help you,' said the youngest son.
And he chopped wood all afternoon.

The woman worked on and on.
Day after day. Night after night.
Sometimes it was too difficult.
Sometimes she cried and her tears
fell onto the cloth. Then she wove
the tears into a river. Sometimes
her fingers bled. Then she wove
the drops of red blood into blood-red
flowers.

Her eyes were tired. She wanted to
close them. But she kept them open
and worked on. Then one night, at
last, it was ready.

'Oh, Mother!' cried her three sons.
'It's beautiful! It's so beautiful!'

Then suddenly a wind came. It blew through the window and it lifted up the brocade.

'Oh!' cried the woman. 'My brocade! My work!'

She tried to catch it. Her sons ran outside and tried to catch it too. But the wind lifted the brocade up high. It blew the brocade high into the sky. And then the wind blew it away.

The woman became ill. She lay in bed for many days and she could not speak. So the youngest son made her some soup. He spoke to her softly and she drank some.

'Are you feeling better?' he asked softly. 'Do you like the soup?'

But all she said was, 'Go to the mountains. Find my brocade and bring it back to me.'

The youngest son told his brothers, and the oldest son went off to find his mother's brocade.

The oldest son walked quickly and
soon he reached the mountains.
Half way up the mountain,
he saw an old woman.
She was sitting under
a cherry tree.

'Where are you going?' she asked.
'I am looking for my mother's brocade,' he said.
'Oh!' she said. 'The brocade! The fairies have it.
The fairies of Sun Mountain. They are copying it.'
'Well, my mother wants it back!' said the oldest son.
'Does she? Then listen!' said the old woman. 'Take
this hammer. Knock out your two front teeth. Give
them to this stone horse. He will eat some cherries
and then you can get onto his back and ride him.
You will have to ride through fire and you will
have to ride through ice.'

The oldest son looked at the hammer and he was afraid. He did not want to knock out his two front teeth. He did not want to ride through fire. He did not want to ride through ice. And … he did not believe her.

'I can't!' he said, at last.

The old woman was kind to him. 'OK,' she said. 'Go home then. Here! Take this bag of coins for your mother. I know that she is poor.'

The oldest son took the bag of coins and thanked the old woman. But he did not go home. He went to a nearby town and spent all the money.

The oldest son did not come home. His mother
waited, but he did not return. So the middle son went
to find the brocade. He walked quickly. Half way up
the mountain he saw the same old woman, sitting
under the cherry tree.

'Where are you going?' she asked him.

'I am looking for my mother's brocade,' he said.

'Oh! The brocade!' she said. 'The fairies have it.
The fairies of Sun Mountain. They are copying it.'

The middle son looked at the old woman. 'Well,
my mother wants to have it back!' he said.

'Then listen!' said the old woman. 'Take this hammer. Knock out your two front teeth. Give them to this stone horse. He will eat some cherries and then you can get on his back and ride him. You will have to ride through fire and you will have to ride through ice.'

The middle son looked at the hammer and he was afraid. He did not want to knock out his two front teeth. He did not want to ride through fire. He did not want to ride through ice. And … he did not believe her.

'I can't,' he said, at last.

Again, the old woman was kind. She gave him a bag of coins for his mother and she told him to go home.

13

The middle son took the bag of coins and thanked
the old woman. But he did not go home. He went to
a nearby town and spent all the money.

His mother waited for him. She
cried so much that her eyes were
red. But he never came.

'Don't cry, Mother,' said the
youngest son. 'Please don't cry
any more. I will go. I will get your
beautiful brocade. Wait for me and
believe in me, because I will bring
it back home to you.'

The youngest son walked quickly and soon he came to the mountains.

Half way up the mountain the youngest son saw the same old woman sitting under the cherry tree. And beside her was the stone horse.

'Where are you going?' she asked, as before.

'I am looking for my mother's brocade,' he said.

'Oh! The brocade!' she said. 'The fairies have it! The fairies of Sun Mountain. They are copying it because it is so beautiful!'

'Well, my mother wants to have it back,' said the youngest son. 'And I have come to get it.'

15

'Then listen!' said the old woman. 'Take this hammer. Knock out your two front teeth. Give them to this stone horse. He will eat some of these cherries, and when he has eaten them you will be able to get on his back and ride him. Be brave. You will have to ride through fire and you will have to ride through ice.'

The youngest son looked at the hammer. He was afraid. He did not want to knock out his two front teeth. He did not want to ride through fire. He did not want to ride through ice. But … he believed her.

'Give me the hammer!' he said. And he knocked out his two front teeth.

The youngest son gave his two front teeth to the stone horse, and at once it was alive! The horse got bigger and it reached up and ate some cherries from the tree. Then it was ready to go.

The youngest son got onto the horse and rode away. He rode quickly and soon he came to Fire Mountain. He stared at it and he was afraid, but he said nothing. He only rode.

He rode towards it and into the fire. The whole place was red hot. There were flames on either side of him, but he did not cry out. He made no sound. Quickly he rode to the top of the mountain and down the other side. He could hear his heart and the sound of the flames. But he said nothing.

Then he came to a huge sea. It was a huge sea
of cold water and ice. The waves were big and
rough, and pieces of ice were crashing around. It
was dangerous and cold. He stared at it and he was
afraid, but he said nothing. He only rode towards it
and through the crashing pieces of ice.

The whole place was icy cold and there was ice on
either side of him. But he did not cry out. Quickly he
rode through it and out to the other side. He could
hear his heart and the sound of the ice breaking,
but he said nothing.

18

The youngest son's clothes were wet. His hair was wet. Water dripped from his clothes and it dripped from his hair.

He sat on the horse and looked in front of him. Ahead, in the soft golden light, he saw a lovely mountain. And at the top of the mountain there was the crystal palace of the fairies of Sun Mountain.

He stared at it for some time because it was so beautiful. Then he rode towards it.

The door to the palace was open. So the youngest son walked into the main hall. Sunlight came through the crystal glass roof and through the big windows. The hall was huge and full of light. Sunlight fell through the glass windows and made little rainbows on the floor.

The whole room was full of the most beautiful light. And the youngest son saw a hundred fairies copying his mother's brocade.

The youngest son walked to the front of the hall.
The fairies all stopped working and looked up at him.

'Good morning!' he said. 'I have come to get my
mother's brocade!'

Nobody said anything. Then a fairy in a red dress
came up to him and touched him on the arm.

'We will soon be finished,' she said softly. 'Then
you can take your mother's brocade back home
to her. But first, go through into the other room.
Eat, drink, and rest yourself. We need to work a
little longer. Tonight we will be finished, and then
tomorrow morning you can take back the brocade.'

The youngest son was hungry and tired. So he thanked the fairy and went into the next room to eat and rest.

There was food on the table and a place where he could sleep. Through the windows he could see the sky and it was beautiful. He lay down and stared at it for several hours.

The fairies worked all day and into the evening. Stars came out in the sky and shone through the crystal glass windows. At last the youngest son's eyes closed and he fell asleep.

Night came. The hundred fairies finished their
work. Now there were a hundred copies of the
brocade. One by one the fairies left the room.

But one fairy did not leave. It was the fairy in
the red dress. She did not want to leave the brocade.
Then, suddenly, she thought of something. She had
an idea. Quietly and carefully she added a picture
of herself to the brocade. She wove herself standing
under a little tree in the garden.

'Now I am a part of the brocade,' she thought.
'So the brocade and I will always be together.'

When morning came, the youngest son woke
up. He was not tired any more. He felt good
and alive. So he went into the hall and got his
mother's brocade.

The fairy in the red dress also woke up early.
'You are taking it away now, aren't you?' she said.

'Yes,' he replied.

'Please thank your mother,' she said. 'Tell her that
we have made a hundred copies.'

'I will,' said the youngest son. He looked at the
fairy. She was so beautiful. He wanted to stay and
talk to her. He wanted to go out onto the mountain
with her and walk in the sunshine, but he had to go.
His mother was waiting. He had to go home.

His mother was waiting. She saw her son and ran out to meet him. She knew that he had the brocade.

And then the strangest thing happened. When he opened the brocade to show his mother, the brocade began to get bigger. A little wind came from somewhere and pulled at the brocade. And the brocade got bigger and bigger.

And then, suddenly, everything came to life! The house and garden became real. The little white and gold house! The beautiful garden full of flowers and trees! They were real!

The mother and her youngest son stood there. They stood there in the garden. All around them were flowers, and then the youngest son saw someone. It was the fairy! The beautiful fairy in the red dress! She was standing under a little tree.

And so it was real. It was all real. The house, the
flowers, the fairy … Everything!

The youngest son married the beautiful fairy and
they all lived happily together in the white and
gold house. The woman no longer wove brocades.
Instead, she spent all her time growing flowers in
the beautiful garden.

Then, one day, two men came down the road. It was the two older brothers. All their money was gone, and they were poor and had nowhere to go. They were sorry for spending the coins and leaving their mother.

'Brothers!' cried the youngest son. 'Look! Look at our beautiful new house! Isn't it wonderful! Brothers! Come home!'

# Exercises

**1  Write the words and find the name of something in the story.**

**2  Make sentences about the story. Then number them 1–6.**

| | |
|---|---|
| ☐ The oldest son went to the mountains … | because it was so beautiful. |
| 1 A woman gave an old man three coins … | because the wind blew her brocade away. |
| ☐ The woman wanted to copy the picture … | because she wanted to buy a picture. |
| ☐ The middle son went to a nearby town … | because the old woman gave him a bag of coins. |
| ☐ The woman became ill … | because he did not believe the old woman. |
| ☐ The oldest son did not take the hammer … | because he wanted to find his mother's brocade. |

**3 Complete the sentences with the past tense of these verbs.**

weave   be   have   add   leave   ~~be~~   think

The hundred fairies finished their work. Now there ___*were*___ a hundred copies of the brocade. One by one the fairies __________ the room.

But one fairy did not leave. It __________ the fairy in the red dress. She did not want to leave the brocade. Then, suddenly, she __________ of something. She __________ an idea. Quietly and carefully she __________ a picture of herself to the brocade. She __________ herself standing under a little tree in the garden.

**4 Match, then write a sentence under each picture.**

saw                     'Come home!'

took away               the beautiful fairy

He

rode                    the brocade

said                    through fire and ice

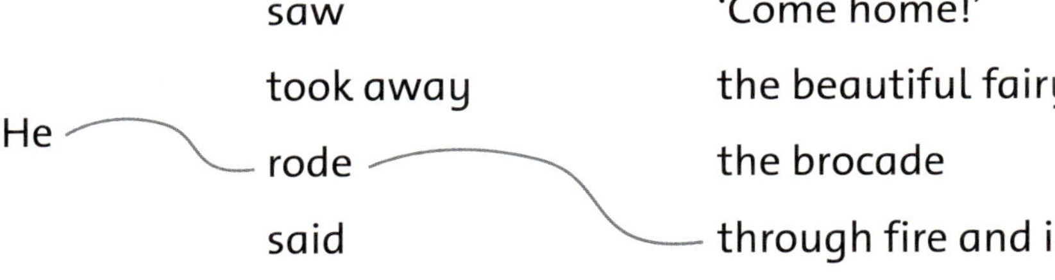

*He rode through fire and ice.* __________________

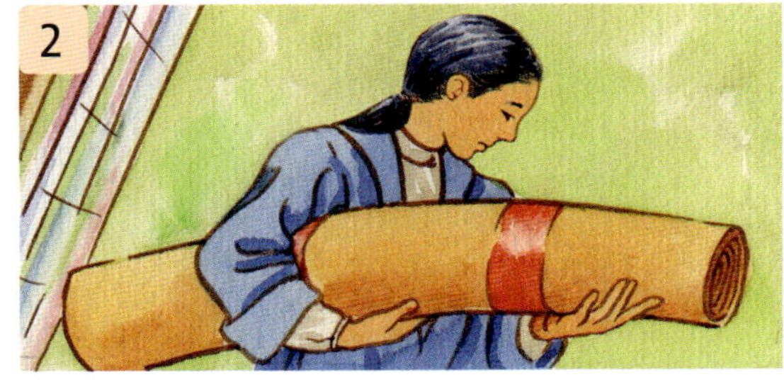

__________________   __________________

# Glossary

**bled** past tense of **bleed**

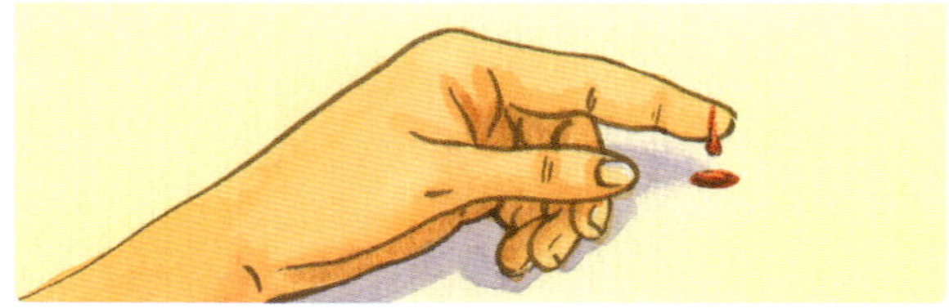

**blew** past tense of **blow**

**brave** not afraid of things

**brocade**

**cherries**

**chop**

**cloth**

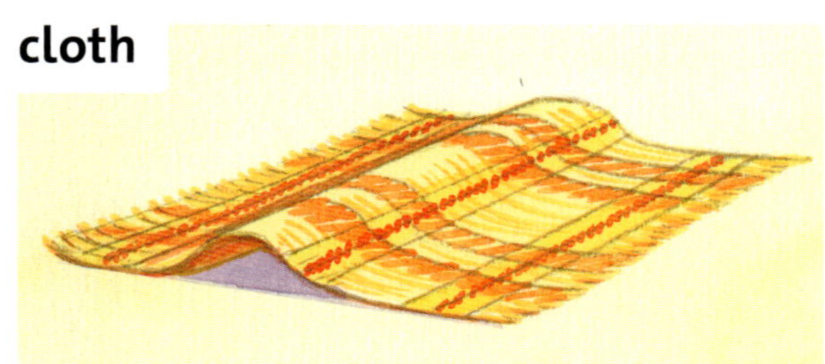

**coin**

**copy** to make something that is like something else

**crystal**

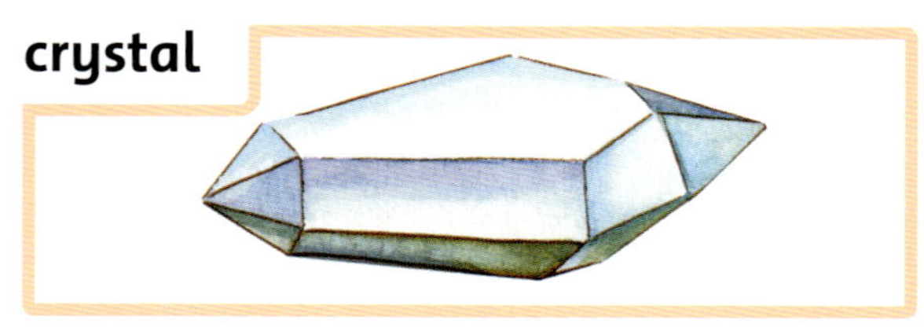

**dripped** past tense of **drip**

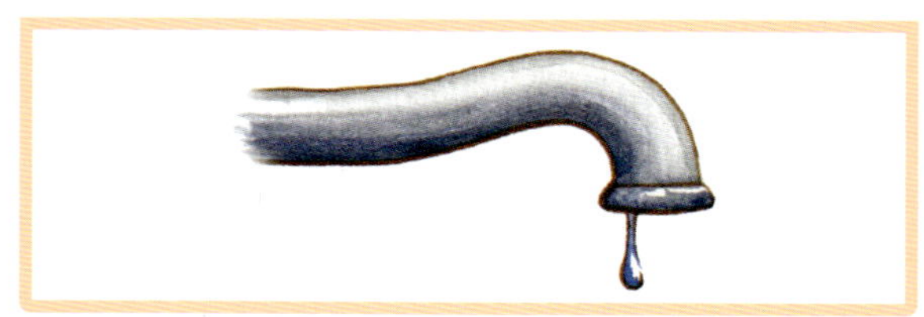

**fairy**

**flames**  parts of a fire; you see them when something is burning

**flour**  you use it to make bread / cakes

**hall**  a large room where people meet

**hammer**

**heart**  it makes blood move around the body

**ice**  water that is frozen (made cold so it turns hard)

**knock out**  to hit something and make it come out

**lifted**  past tense of **lift**: to move something up off eg a floor / table

**market**  an outdoor place in a town where people buy or sell things

**palace**  a king or queen's home

**rainbow**

**rice**

**roof**  a cover on a building

**soup**  food that you can drink; it is made from vegetables or meat cooked in water

**stared**  past tense of **stare**: to look at something for a long time

**stone**  a hard thing from the ground; you can build with it

**tear**  water that comes from your eyes when you cry

**village**  a very small town in the country

**waves**

**wood**  hard material that comes from trees

**wove**  past tense of **weave**: to make cloth from eg cotton / wool

# Classic Tales

Classic stories retold for learners of English – bringing the magic of traditional storytelling to the language classroom

### Level 1: 100 headwords

- The Enormous Turnip
- The Little Red Hen
- Lownu Mends the Sky
- The Magic Cooking Pot
- Mansour and the Donkey
- Peach Boy
- The Princess and the Pea
- Rumpelstiltskin
- The Shoemaker and the Elves
- Three Billy-Goats

### Level 2: 150 headwords

- Amrita and the Trees
- Big Baby Finn
- The Fisherman and his Wife
- The Gingerbread Man
- Jack and the Beanstalk
- Thumbelina
- The Town Mouse and the Country Mouse
- The Ugly Duckling

### Level 3: 200 headwords

- Aladdin
- Goldilocks and the Three Bears
- The Little Mermaid
- Little Red Riding Hood

### Level 4: 300 headwords

- Cinderella
- The Goose Girl
- Sleeping Beauty
- The Twelve Dancing Princesses

### Level 5: 400 headwords

- Beauty and the Beast
- The Magic Brocade
- Pinocchio
- Snow White and the Seven Dwarfs

All *Classic Tales* have an accompanying

- **e-Book with Audio Pack** containing the book and the e-book with audio, for use on a computer or CD player. Teachers can also project the e-book onto an interactive whiteboard to use it like a Big Book.
- **Activity Book and Play** providing extra language practice and the story adapted as a play for performance in class or on stage.

For more details, visit
www.oup.com/elt/readers/classictales



# OXFORD
## UNIVERSITY PRESS

Great Clarendon Street, Oxford, OX2 6DP, United Kingdom

Oxford University Press is a department of the University of Oxford. It furthers the University's objective of excellence in research, scholarship, and education by publishing worldwide. Oxford is a registered trade mark of Oxford University Press in the UK and in certain other countries

© Oxford University Press 2012

The moral rights of the author have been asserted

First published in Classic Tales 2009

2016 2015 2014 2013 2012

10 9 8 7 6 5 4 3 2 1

**No unauthorized photocopying**

All rights reserved. No part of this publication may be reproduced, stored in a retrieval system, or transmitted, in any form or by any means, without the prior permission in writing of Oxford University Press, or as expressly permitted by law, by licence or under terms agreed with the appropriate reprographics rights organization. Enquiries concerning reproduction outside the scope of the above should be sent to the ELT Rights Department, Oxford University Press, at the address above

You must not circulate this work in any other form and you must impose this same condition on any acquirer

Links to third party websites are provided by Oxford in good faith and for information only. Oxford disclaims any responsibility for the materials contained in any third party website referenced in this work

ISBN: 978 0 19 423962 2

This *Classic Tale* title is available as an e-Book with Audio Pack
ISBN: 978 0 19 423965 3

Also available: The Magic Brocade Activity Book and Play
ISBN: 978 0 19 423963 9

Printed in China

This book is printed on paper from certified and well-managed sources.

ACKNOWLEDGEMENTS

*Illustrated by*: Nancy Lane/Melissa Turk & The Artist Network